From the desktop of Jeffrey Simmons

A vacation in Paris inspired Miroslav Sasek to create childrens travel guides to the big cities of the world. He brought me *This is Paris* in 1958, when I was publishing in London, and we soon followed up with *This is London*. Both books were enormously successful, and his simple vision grew to include more than a dozen books. Their amusing verse, coupled with bright and charming illustrations, made for a series unlike any other, and garnered Sasek (as we always called him) the international and popular acclaim he deserved.

I was thrilled to learn that *This is Rome* will once again find its rightful place on book-shelves. Sasek is no longer with us (and I have lost all contact with his family), but I am sure he would be delighted to know that a whole new generation of wide-eyed readers is being introduced to his whimsical, imaginative, and enchanting world.

Your name here

Published by arrangement with Simon & Schuster Books for Young Readers,
Simon & Schuster Children's Publishing Division

This edition first published in the United States of America in 2007 by
UNIVERSE PUBLISHING
A Division of Rizzoli International Publications, Inc.
300 Park Avenue South
New York, NY 10010
www.rizzoliusa.com

*See updated Rome facts at end of book

2010 2011 / 10 9 8 7 6 5 4

Printed in China

ISBN–10: 0-7893-1549-1
ISBN–13: 978-0-7893-1549-6

Library of Congress Control Number: 2006907092

Cover design: centerpointdesign

M · SASEK

THIS · IS · ROME

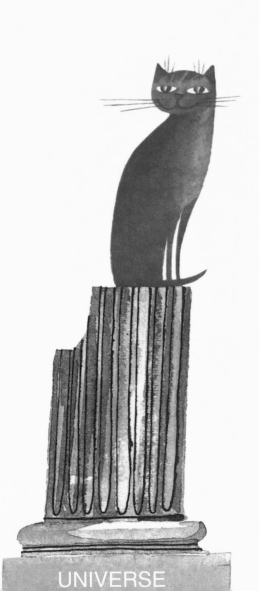

UNIVERSE

Let's go right back to the beginning.

Once upon a time there was a motherly she-wolf and two baby brothers called Romulus and Remus. The wolf brought them up herself. When Romulus was a grown man he founded a village which grew and grew till it became a great city covering seven hills.

And this city was Rome.

According to the legend all this started two thousand seven hundred years ago, right here | on a hill called the Palatine.

The center of the ancient city, called the Forum Romanum, was at the foot of the Palatine Hill. It was full of temples and memorial columns and triumphal arches, and it was here that Mark Antony mourned over the body of Julius Caesar.

And now let's see what Rome looks like today.

A city of laurel wreaths and fountains playing under a bright blue sky. Once the capital of the Roman Empire, now the capital of Italy and the center of Catholic Christendom, Rome is the "eternal city" — where the old world and the new stand side by side.

The ancient Romans looked like this:

Caesar the Dictator

S·P·Q·R·
C·IVLIO CAESARI
DICT·PERPETVO

Rome's first Emperor, Augustus.
He ruled two thousand years ago,
when Rome already had
a million citizens.

S·P·Q·R·
IMP·CAESARI·DIVI·F·
AVGVSTO
PATRI·PATRIAE

The Romans of today look quite different.

Everywhere you see this inscription —

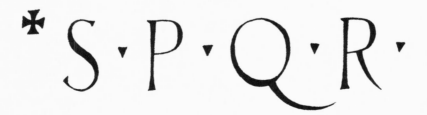

Which stands for SENATUS POPULUSQUE ROMANUS, "The Roman Senate and people." This was the equivalent of the city arms or of modern inscriptions like "London County Council."

The Romanest Romans, they say, are to be found in a crowded quarter of the city called Trastevere.

The blue ribbon means that another little Roman has been born in this house.

The central point of Rome today is the Piazza Venezia, "Venice Square."
At the back stands what some people call the "Wedding Cake" or the "Typewriter" —
but the proper name is the Monument to Victor Emmanuel II. It is only about a century
old; inside is the Tomb of the Unknown Warrior from the First World War.
The Palazzo Venezia on the right was built in the fifteenth century and the Pope used
to live there.

Now we are standing on the top of another of the seven hills — the Capitol.
In ancient Rome the temples of Jupiter and Juno stood here. Today there is the
City Hall, with a museum on each side and the gilt statue of Emperor Marcus
Aurelius in the middle.* The whole square was designed by the great
Renaissance artist Michelangelo.

There are two she-wolves to be seen here:

one is 2300 years old —

and the other 2300 years younger.

And in the courtyard of the museum is a little piece of another great Emperor — Constantine.

It was during Trajan's reign that the Roman Empire reached its greatest extent, from England to Egypt, from Spain to the Caucasus.
This is the Forum Trajanum with the Emperor Trajan's column. It was set up in the second century, with a statue of the Emperor on the top. But later they put a statue of Saint Peter on it instead.

This temple is the Pantheon, two hundred years older even than Trajan's column. These two are the only monuments of ancient Rome that have survived to our day undamaged.

Inside the Pantheon are the tombs of the Kings of Italy — and of another great Renaissance painter, Raphael.

"Rome was not built in a day," but the Colosseum was built in eight years. The work was finished in the year 80, and there was room for 50,000 people to sit inside and watch the gladiators fighting.

But if you go inside today all you see are cats and tourists and photographers and postcard sellers.

The Piazza Bocca della Verità — the Square of the Mouth of Truth:
the Temple of Vesta and the Temple of Fortuna Virilis.

In the Church of Santa Maria in Cosmedin, in the same square, is the
"Mouth of Truth." Stick your hand inside; if you have told a lie, it will bite it off!

A few yards farther on we come to the Tiber River.
This is how they fish in it.*

Many ancient columns have Corinthian capitals carved in a pattern of acanthus leaves. The acanthus plant still grows everywhere in Rome. Here is a single leaf.

The Bridge of Fabricius — the oldest in Rome — leads from the right of this picture on to the city's only island, Isola Tiberina.

The Square of the Knights of Malta lies on another of the seven hills —
the Aventine. If you peep through a little opening in the gate —

you can see right across Rome to the biggest church in the world — Saint Peter's.

Now we have come up quite close to it. We are standing on the edge of Saint Peter's Square in the Vatican City. The Basilica of Saint Peter's stands on the site of the Emperor Nero's Circus, where hundreds of early Christians were martyred, and beneath it, according to tradition, lies the tomb of Saint Peter himself. For two hundred years some of the most famous artists of the Renaissance worked on the building. The dome was designed by Michelangelo, and the Basilica was consecrated by Pope Urban VIII in 1626. The colonnade around the square is in four rows, one behind another, with 284 columns, 88 pillars, and 140 statues. It was designed by Giovanni Lorenzo Bernini.

This is one of the Swiss Guards keeping watch at the entrance to the Vatican, which lies behind the Basilica. The Vatican City, where the Pope lives, has been a sovereign state of its own since 1929 although it has only about five hundred inhabitants.

There are more ancient statues in the Vatican Museums than you will find anywhere else in the world. You have to pass through these museums if you want to reach the Sistine Chapel with Michelangelo's famous frescoes.

The Castle of Sant'Angelo was started by the Emperor Hadrian as a family mausoleum. In the Middle Ages it was turned into a fortress.

In 1527 one of the Popes — Clement VII — fled here from the Vatican through a secret passageway when Rome was being sacked by foreign troops.

The Basilica of San Giovanni in Laterano — it is called the "Mother and Head of all Churches" — was founded by the first Christian Emperor of Rome, Constantine the Great. Destroyed once by an earthquake and twice by fire, it was rebuilt several times until it was finally "modernized" — three hundred years ago.

This is a popular place to have little Romans baptized as you can see for yourself any Sunday morning.

The Palazzo del Laterano — next to the Basilica — was another building where the Popes lived.

Thousands of students from all parts of the world study theology in Rome.

The American students look like this —

the Germans like this —

and the Scots like this.

This is Santa Maria Maggiore.
A legend says that the Virgin Mary appeared in A.D. 352 to Pope Liberius and to a Roman nobleman, Johannes, commanding them to erect a church to her on the exact spot where they were to find snow on the following morning. This was in the heat of a Roman August — but the next day, miraculously, snow fell just here.

These are the "carabinieri" in parade uniform.

The Quirinal Palace was first the summer residence of the Popes and then, after 1870, the Royal Palace. Since World War II Italy has had no kings, and now the President of the Republic lives here.

Inside this church — San Pietro in Vincoli, Saint Peter in Chains —

you can see the Mausoleum of Pope Julius II, with Michelangelo's famous statue of Moses.

Diocletian's Baths, built at the end of the third century after Christ, were the biggest in Rome. Today they form the National Museum of Rome and house all kinds of works of art discovered in the city — Greek, Roman, and Christian.

The Baths of Caracalla are nearly one hundred years older. Nowadays they are used as an open-air theater for summer performances of the Roman Opera.

We are standing on the Via Appia Antica — the Old Appian Way —
built nearly twenty-three centuries ago to join Rome and Capua.
The road is lined with ancient Roman graves, for in those days it was
forbidden to bury people within the City itself.

The earliest burial places of the Christians were the underground
Catacombs. When you go inside them today you are given a candle
at the entrance instead of a ticket.

On the right side of this square, the Piazza di Spagna, is the little building
where the English poet John Keats spent his last days.
The flight of steps leads up to the church of Trinità dei Monti.

As you walk up them you will see that Rome is a city where oranges and lemons ripen in the courtyards —

and palm trees grow on the rooftops.

A few steps away is the Villa Medici, nowadays the French Academy.
And from here you can enjoy a fine view of the whole city.

A little farther on and you find yourself in the Pincio, a public park on the site of the famous gardens of Lucullus.

The sunset seen from here is better than Technicolor — so the guides will tell you.

But the biggest park in Rome is the Borghese Gardens with its own art
gallery. This is the Giardino del Lago —

and this is the main drive up to the whole Gardens.

On the ruins of the Emperor Domitian's Stadium arose the Piazza Navona
with all its fountains. The one in the middle is by Bernini. The obelisk was
taken from the Circus of Maxentius on the Via Appia.

Another Roman square, the Piazza Sant'Ignazio,
looks just like a stage setting.

This pyramid is the funeral monument of a magistrate, Caius Cestius, who died in 12 B.C. Behind it lies the Protestant Cemetery, where you can see the tombs of Keats and Shelley.

Another pyramid — bottles of Chianti, the Italian red wine.

Here are some Roman trams,
buses and trolleybuses.*

A Roman taxi —

and the Roman underground.

In the park there is another way to get around — on donkey-back.

Rome is full of statues, but full of motorcycles too. We prefer the statues; they are so much quieter.

And this is . . .

Termini, the main station in Rome, where all Roman Holidays begin and end.

But perhaps you wish it were not going to be your last holiday in Rome.
So take a ride on your last evening in one of these ancient coaches —

and drive to the biggest and most famous of Roman fountains,
the Fontana di Trevi.

Step down here and throw in a coin.

If you do it the right way — turning your back and throwing it over your right shoulder — you can be sure that one day you will come back.

There's one thing, of course — you can never miss your way. For wherever you come from, all roads lead to Rome!

THIS IS ROME . . . TODAY!

*Page 16: Today the statue is a copy; the restored original is on display in the Capitoline Museums.

*Page 23: Today fishermen are a rare sight; the river is quite polluted.

*Page 52: Today trolleybuses, after disappearing in 1972, have returned to Rome.